I Can Make
JEWELRY

written and photographed by

Mary Wallace

Owl Books

I Can Make Jewelry

Owl Books are published by Greey de Pencier Books Inc.,
179 John Street, Suite 500, Toronto, Ontario M5T 3G5

Owl and the Owl colophon are trademarks of Owl Communications.
Greey de Pencier Books Inc. is a licensed user of trademarks of Owl Communications.

Distributed in the United States by Firefly Books (U.S.) Inc.,
230 Fifth Avenue, Suite 1607, New York, NY 10001.

This book was published with the generous support of the Canada Council,
the Ontario Arts Council and the Government of Ontario through
the Ontario Publishing Centre.

Cataloguing in Publication Data

Wallace, Mary, 1950–
I can make jewelry

ISBN 1-895688-62-0 (bound)
ISBN 1-895688-63-9 (pbk.)

1. Jewelry making – Juvenile literature.
I. Title.

TT212.W35 1997   j745.594'2   C96-931440-X

Design & Art Direction: Julia Naimska

Jewelry on the front cover, counterclockwise from upper left:
Crescent Moon Pin; Ribbon Wrap hairband; Hands to Hold; Laced-up Locket; Daisy Chain bracelets; Rainbow Necklace.

Other books by Mary Wallace
I Can Make Toys
I Can Make Puppets
I Can Make Gifts
I Can Make Games
I Can Make Nature Crafts
I Can Make Costumes
I Can Make Art
How to Make Great Stuff to Wear
How to Make Great Stuff for Your Room

Printed in Hong Kong

A   B   C   D   E   F

CONTENTS

LET'S MAKE JEWELRY

You can make and wear all the jewelry in this book. It's easy. It's fun. These two pages show the things used to make everything here, but you can use other things if you like. You'll find most of what you need around the house — remember to get permission to use what you find.

- acrylic paint
- Bristol board
- buttons
- fishing line
- beads
- aluminum foil
- bead string
- barrette
- star confetti
- chalk
- ballpoint pen
- cardboard

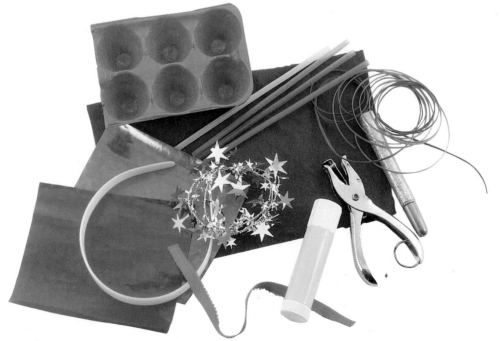

- egg carton
- drinking straws
- shiny paper
- hairband
- star garland
- elastic
- glue stick
- hole punch
- glitter glue
- gimp or lanyard
- knit fabric

- sequins
- safety pin
- paper clips
- sandpaper
- masking tape
- pencil crayons
- pipe cleaners
- light fabric
- markers
- paint brush

- plastic container
- polyester stuffing
- plastic container lid
- ribbon
- rubber band
- scissors
- shiny odds and ends

- shoe box
- long sock or tights
- stones
- tracing paper
- white glue
- shoelaces
- twist ties
- yarn
- tape

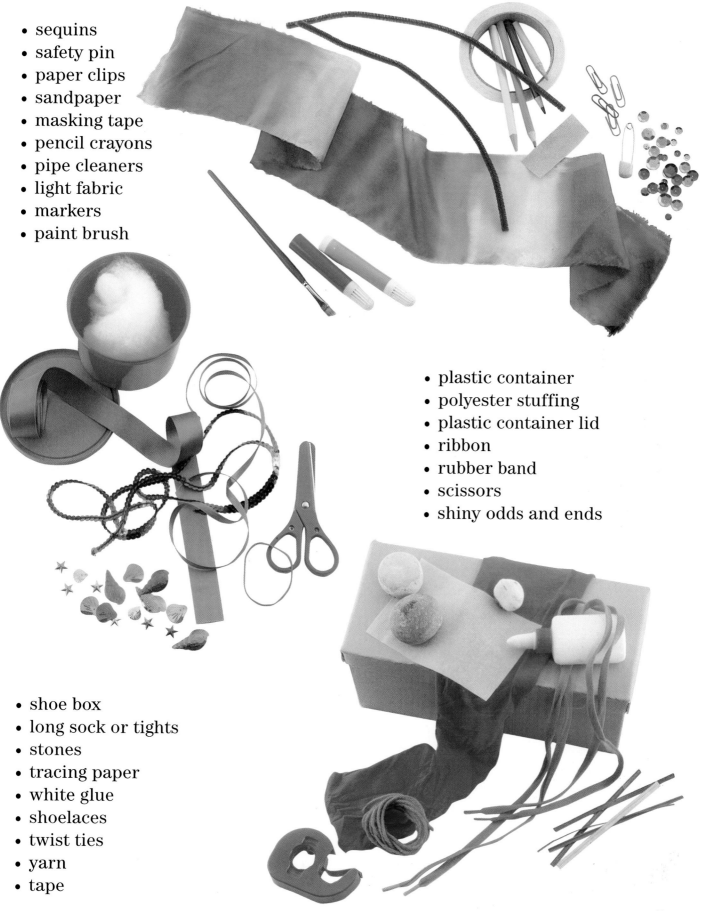

HANDS TO HOLD

- tracing paper
- scissors
- pencil
- ballpoint pen
- plastic container lid
- hole punch
- ribbon or yarn
- *grown-up to help*

pattern

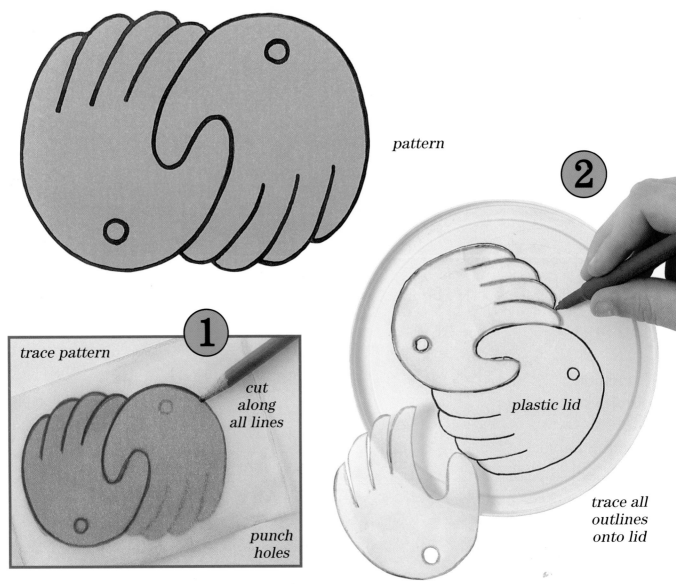

1 trace pattern

cut along all lines

punch holes

2 plastic lid

trace all outlines onto lid

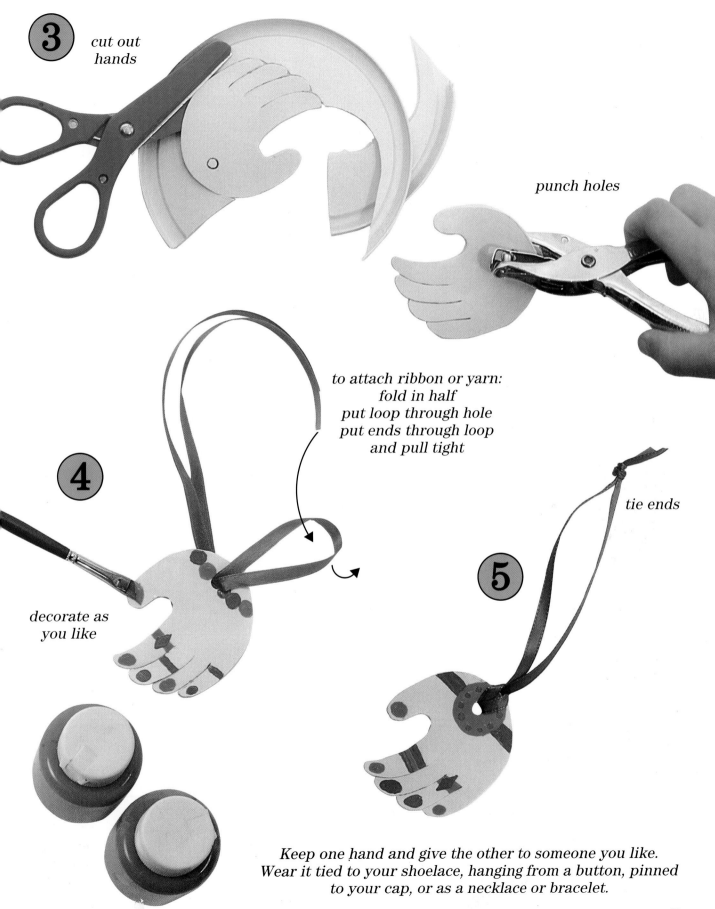

3 *cut out hands*

punch holes

to attach ribbon or yarn:
fold in half
put loop through hole
put ends through loop
and pull tight

4

decorate as you like

5

tie ends

Keep one hand and give the other to someone you like. Wear it tied to your shoelace, hanging from a button, pinned to your cap, or as a necklace or bracelet.

RINGS 'N' THINGS

RINGS

- buttons and beads
- yarn
- scissors

(**1**) run yarn through bead or button

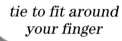 *tie to fit around your finger*

 knot

trim ends

(**2**)

EARRINGS

- drinking straws
- scissors
- rings (see above or use any ring)

(**1**) *cut small pieces of straw*

(**2**) *snip open as shown*

(**3**) *slide ring onto straw*

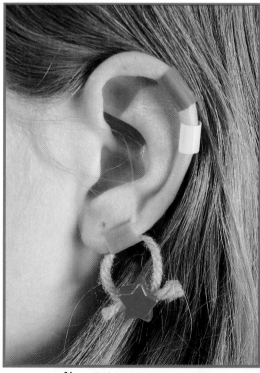

clip straw on your ear

HANDSTAND

- corrugated cardboard
- pencil
- scissors
- acrylic paint and brush
- *grown-up to help*

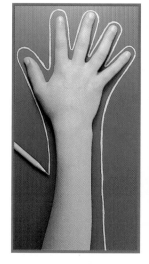

trace hand
on cardboard

draw a wide base

3

draw a triangle
on cardboard

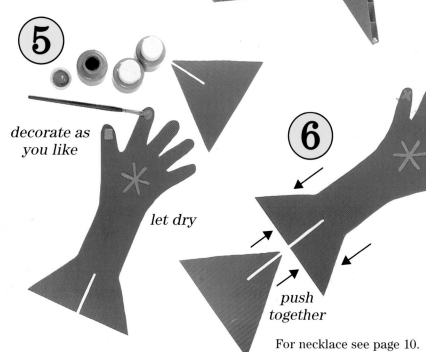

4

cut
out

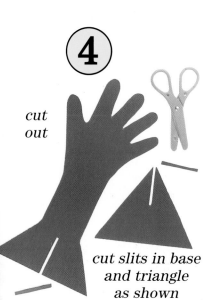

cut slits in base
and triangle
as shown

5

decorate as
you like

let dry

6

push
together

For necklace see page 10. 9

FRIENDS ALL AROUND

- drinking straws
- scissors
- twist ties
- tape
- piece of yarn

①

for each friend, cut five long pieces and one short piece of straw

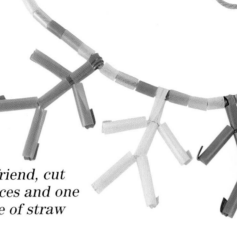

②

fold two twist ties in half

③

make loop

push short straw piece onto folded end for head

④

bend arms out

use a long straw piece for body

⑤

push long straw pieces onto arms

bend legs out

⑥

push long straw pieces onto legs

trim and fold ends up

make more friends

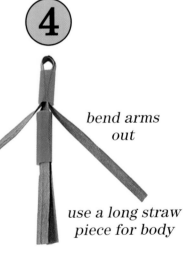

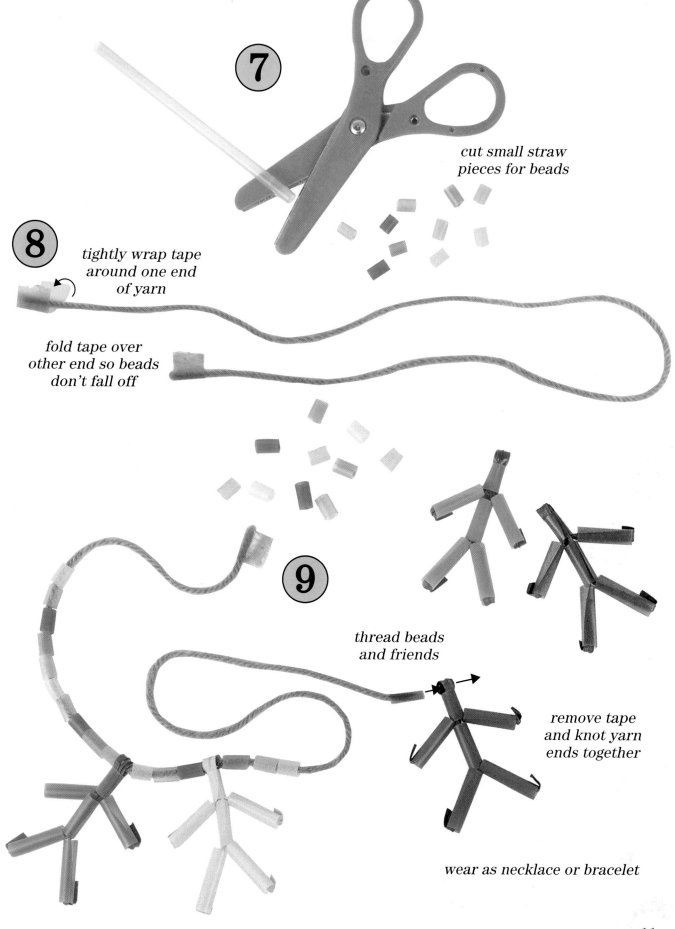

7 cut small straw pieces for beads

8 tightly wrap tape around one end of yarn

fold tape over other end so beads don't fall off

9 thread beads and friends

remove tape and knot yarn ends together

wear as necklace or bracelet

SUPER SCRUNCHIE

- long sock or one leg from tights
- scissors
- elastic

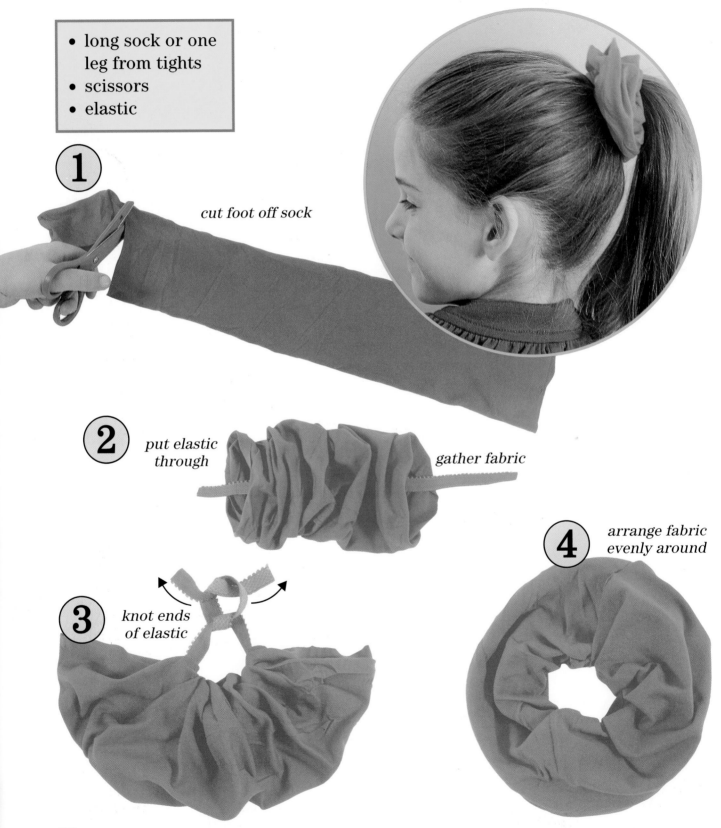

1 cut foot off sock

2 put elastic through   gather fabric

3 knot ends of elastic

4 arrange fabric evenly around

RIBBON WRAP

- hairband
- white glue
- scissors
- ribbon
- bead string
- glitter glue

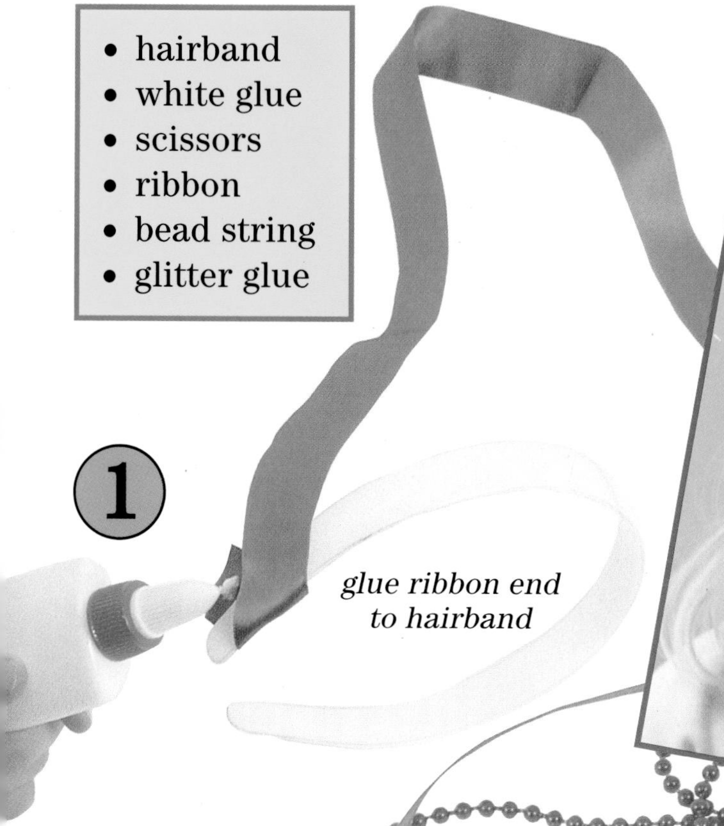

1 glue ribbon end to hairband

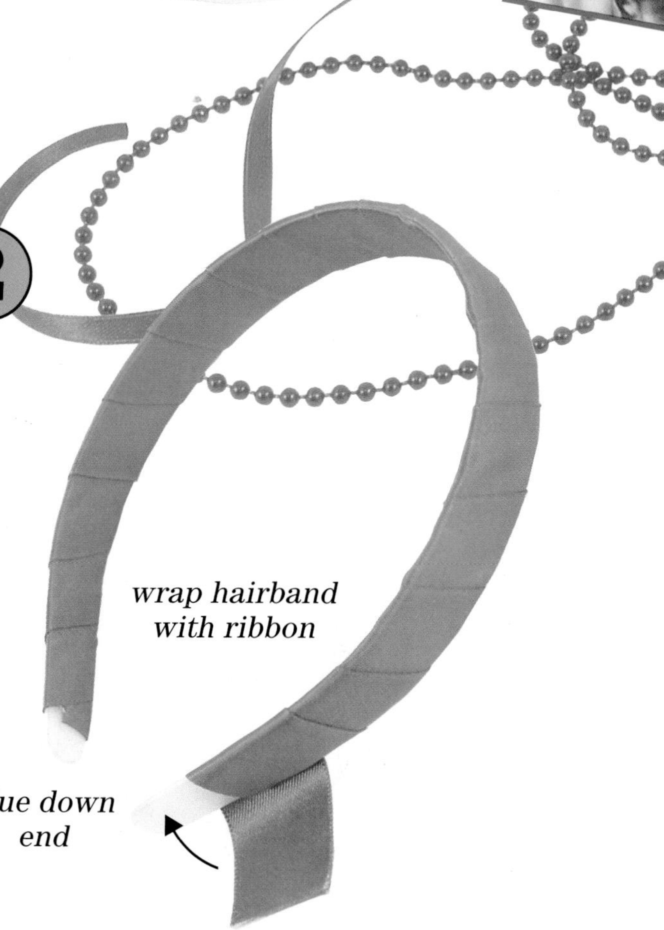

2 wrap hairband with ribbon

glue down end

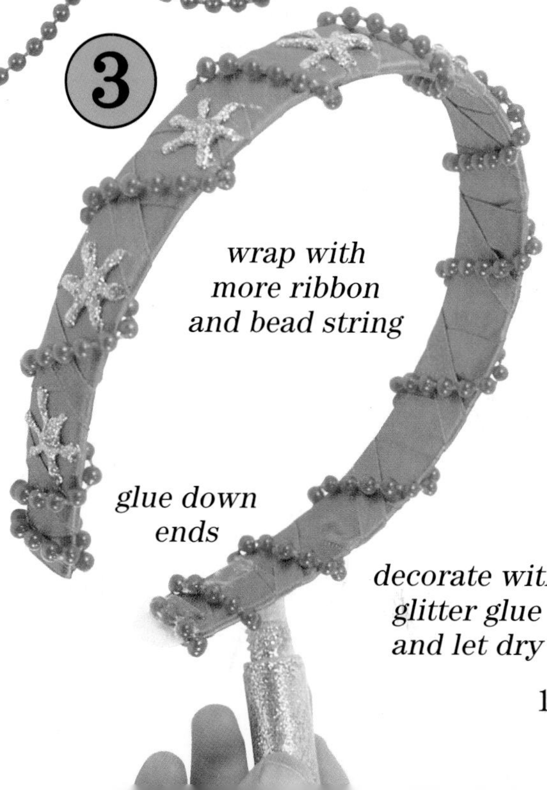

3 wrap with more ribbon and bead string

glue down ends

decorate with glitter glue and let dry

13

LADYBUG BROOCH

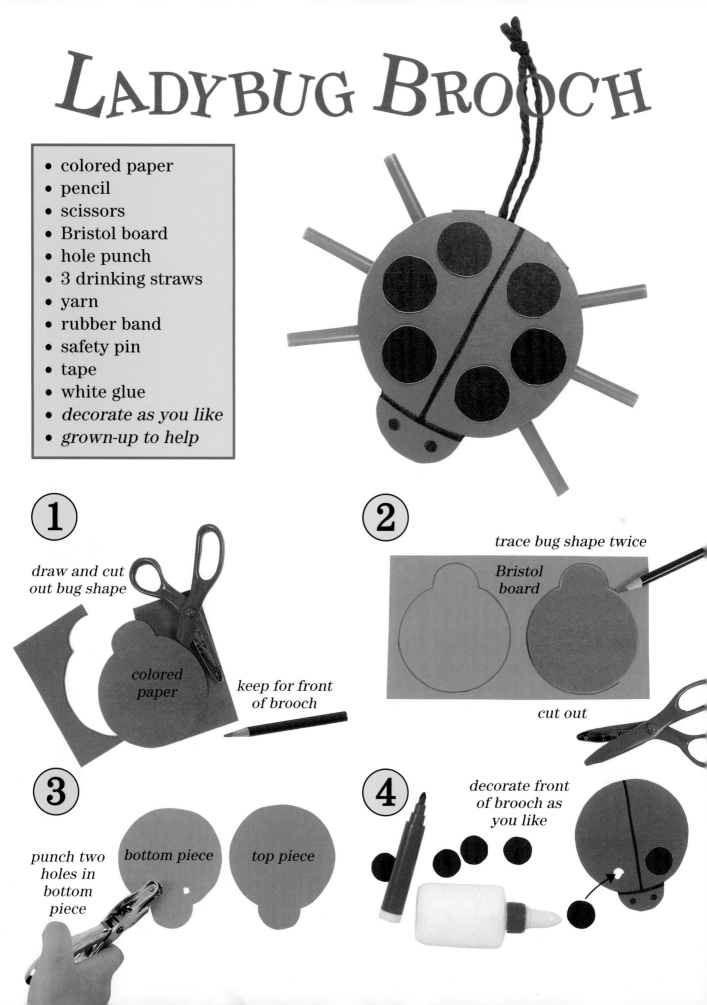

- colored paper
- pencil
- scissors
- Bristol board
- hole punch
- 3 drinking straws
- yarn
- rubber band
- safety pin
- tape
- white glue
- *decorate as you like*
- *grown-up to help*

1

draw and cut out bug shape

colored paper

keep for front of brooch

2

trace bug shape twice

Bristol board

cut out

3

punch two holes in bottom piece

bottom piece

top piece

4

decorate front of brooch as you like

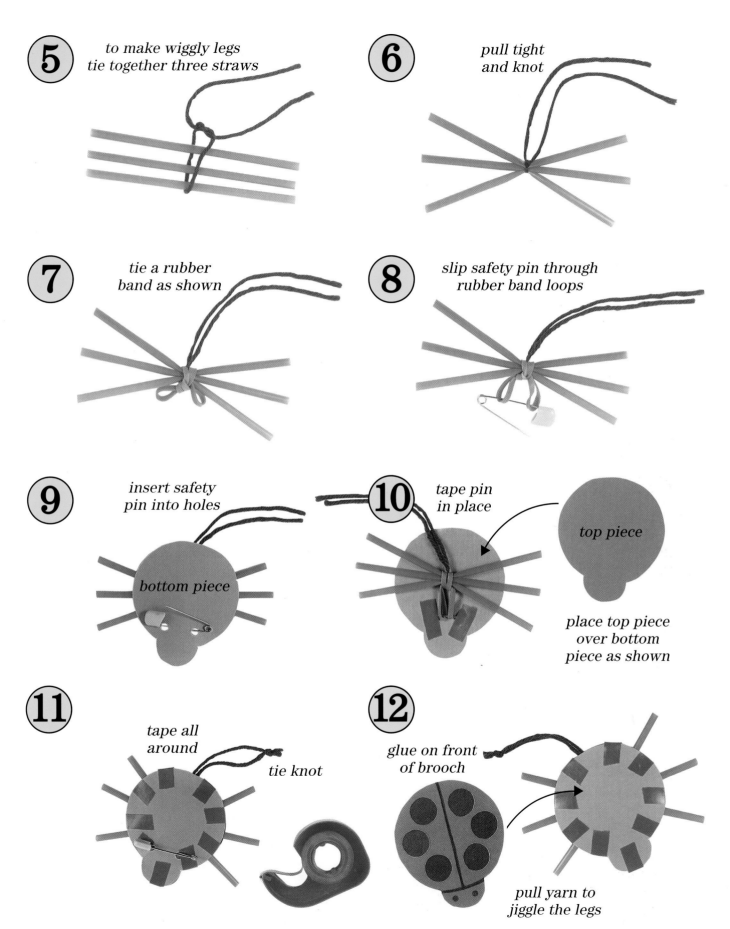

5 to make wiggly legs tie together three straws

6 pull tight and knot

7 tie a rubber band as shown

8 slip safety pin through rubber band loops

9 insert safety pin into holes

bottom piece

10 tape pin in place

top piece

place top piece over bottom piece as shown

11 tape all around

tie knot

12 glue on front of brooch

pull yarn to jiggle the legs

BEAUTIFUL BEADING

on fishing line   *for beads with small holes*

on gimp or lanyard   *fold tape at other end to prevent beads from falling off*

on yarn   *wrap tape around one end for easy threading*

on shoelaces   *for beads with large holes*

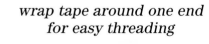

16

For straw pieces as beads see page 10.

1-2-3 Beaded Belt

- 2 shoelaces long enough to tie loosely around your waist
- beads with large holes (around 200)

1 *pull 2 shoe laces together through 1 bead*

2 *separate the laces and thread 3 beads on each*

3 *thread a bead onto one lace, then the second lace*

4 *pull laces so beads fit snugly against each other*

5 *repeat steps 2 to 4 in both directions until the beads go around your waist, then knot lace ends*

tie around your waist with a loose knot

DAISY CHAINS

- beads with large holes in 3 colors: blue, pink and dark pink are shown here
- long piece of gimp or lanyard

thread one blue bead onto end

knot loosely to hold in place

①

②

add more blue beads

③

thread 7 pink beads

18

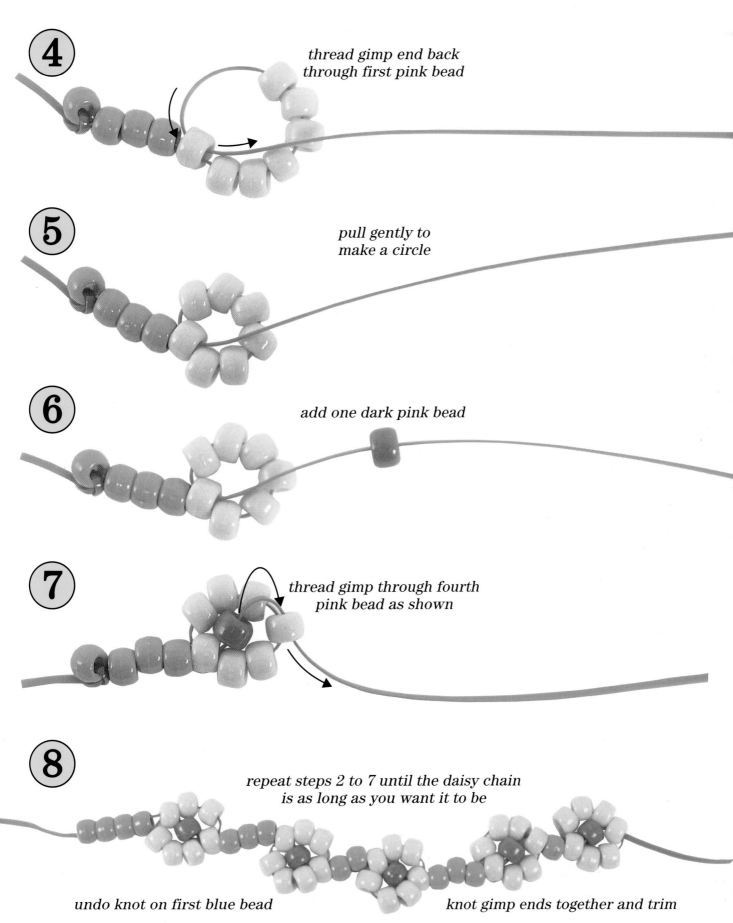

4 *thread gimp end back through first pink bead*

5 *pull gently to make a circle*

6 *add one dark pink bead*

7 *thread gimp through fourth pink bead as shown*

8 *repeat steps 2 to 7 until the daisy chain is as long as you want it to be*

undo knot on first blue bead

knot gimp ends together and trim

Sun Barrette

- tracing paper
- ballpoint pen
- scissors
- hole punch
- plastic container
- masking tape
- yarn
- button or bead
- pencil with point sanded off
- white glue
- *grown-up to help*

1 *trace pattern onto paper*

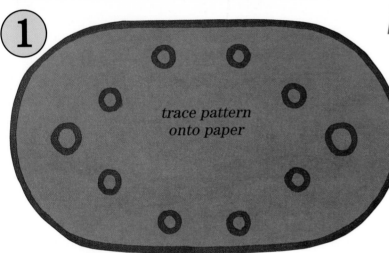

2 *cut out*

punch holes

3 *trace* *tape*

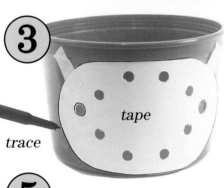

4 *cut out and punch holes*

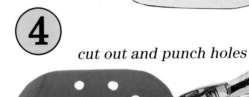

punch end holes larger

5 *lace yarn as shown with button on top*

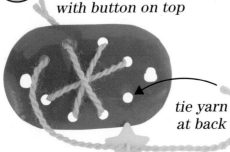

tie yarn at back

6 *cover pencil end with glue and let dry*

7 *slide pencil through end holes*

STAR BARRETTE

- barrette
- bead string
- star garland
- ribbon
- shiny leaves

1 tie end of ribbon to barrette

2 make loops with bead string and wind tightly with ribbon

3 make loops with star garland and wind tightly with ribbon

4 stick leaves into ribbon loops

tie ribbon end to barrette

LACED-UP LOCKET

- tracing paper
- pencil
- scissors
- Bristol board
- hole punch
- yarn
- photo
- white glue
- large bead
- *decorate as you like*
- *grown-up to help*

1 *trace whole pattern onto tracing paper*

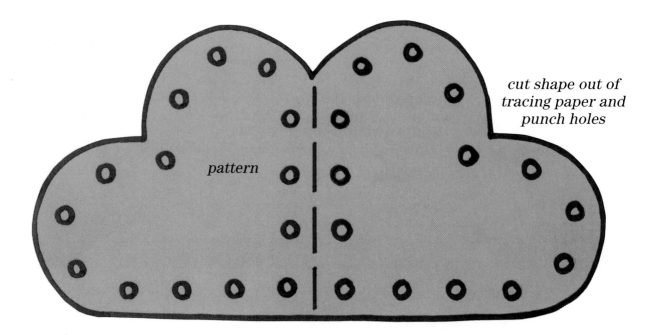

pattern

cut shape out of tracing paper and punch holes

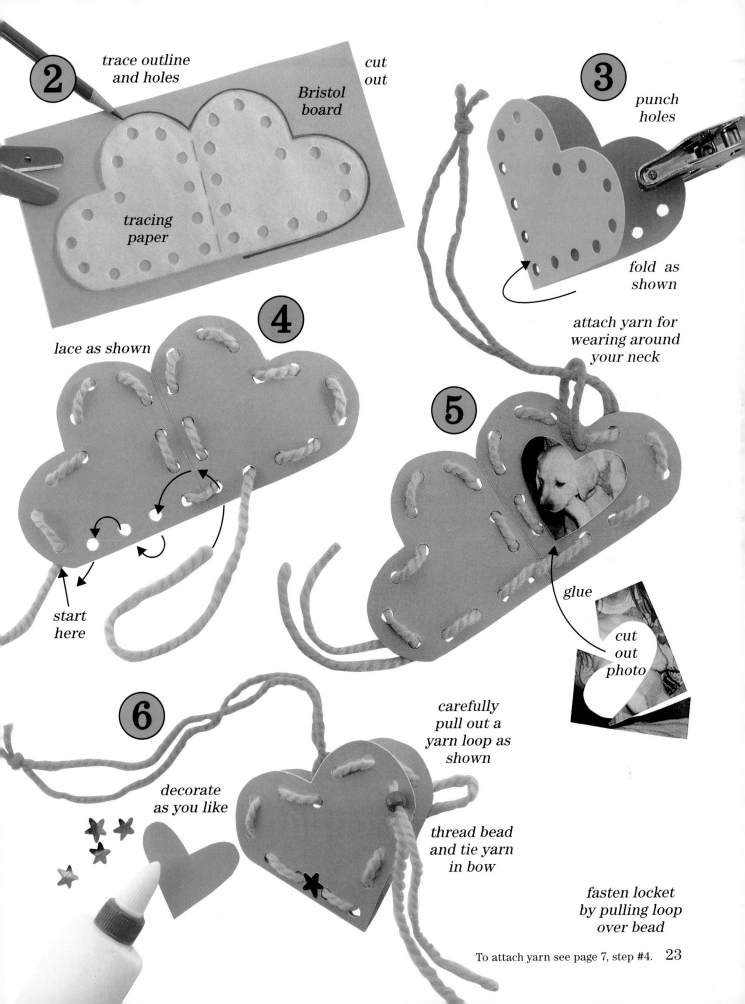

2 trace outline and holes

cut out

Bristol board

tracing paper

3 punch holes

fold as shown

attach yarn for wearing around your neck

4 lace as shown

start here

5 glue

cut out photo

carefully pull out a yarn loop as shown

thread bead and tie yarn in bow

fasten locket by pulling loop over bead

6 decorate as you like

To attach yarn see page 7, step #4. 23

STARRY EYES

- egg carton
- scissors
- hole punch
- pipe cleaners
- shiny paper
- sequins
- white glue
- *grown-up to help*

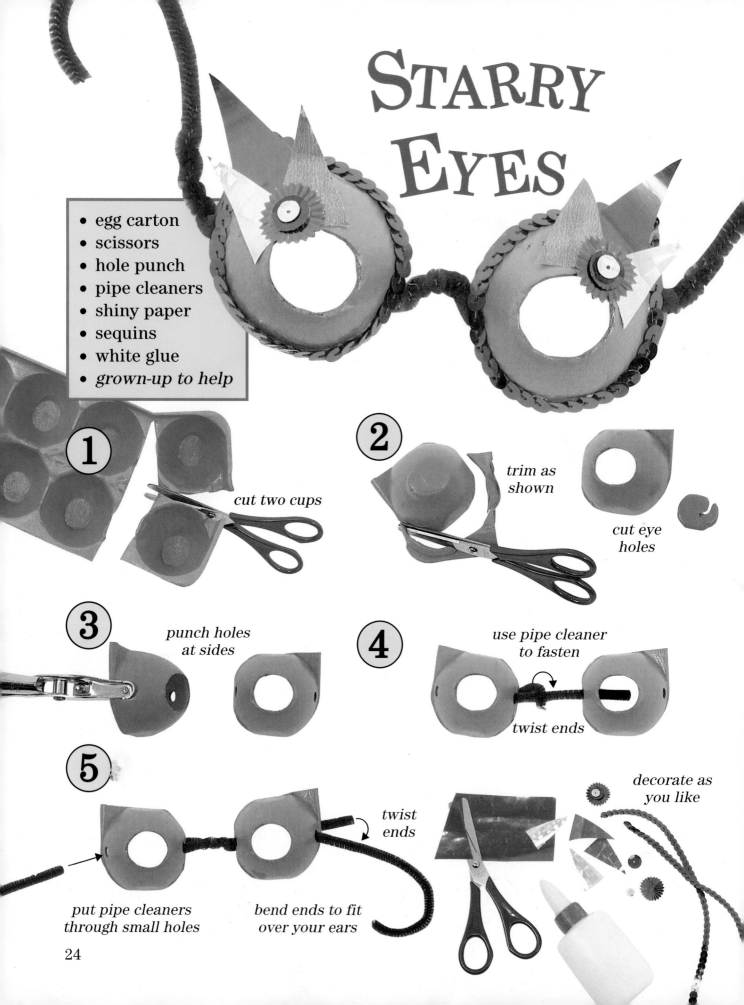

1 cut two cups

2 trim as shown — cut eye holes

3 punch holes at sides

4 use pipe cleaner to fasten — twist ends

5 put pipe cleaners through small holes — bend ends to fit over your ears — twist ends — decorate as you like

CRESCENT MOON PIN

- cardboard
- pencil
- scissors
- hole punch
- safety pin
- masking tape
- paper clips
- *grown-up to help*

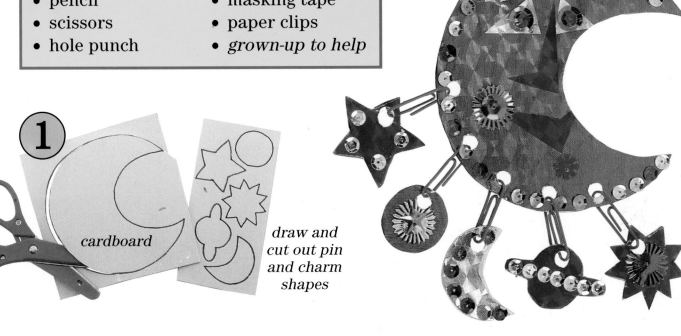

1 *cardboard*

draw and cut out pin and charm shapes

2 *punch two holes*

3 *put safety pin through as shown*

4 *tape*

5 *decorate as you like*

punch holes as shown

6 *slip charms onto paper clips and attach to pin*

RAINBOW NECKLACE

- strip of light fabric
- glue stick
- scissors
- polyester stuffing
- pencil
- beads with large holes

1 *glue one edge of fabric strip*

2 *fold lengthwise and glue down edge*   *let dry*

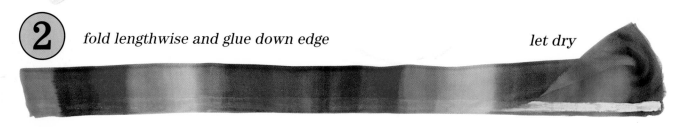

3 *trim to make pointed ends*

4 *open one end of tube and place a small ball of stuffing inside*

5 *gently push stuffing to middle of tube with a pencil*

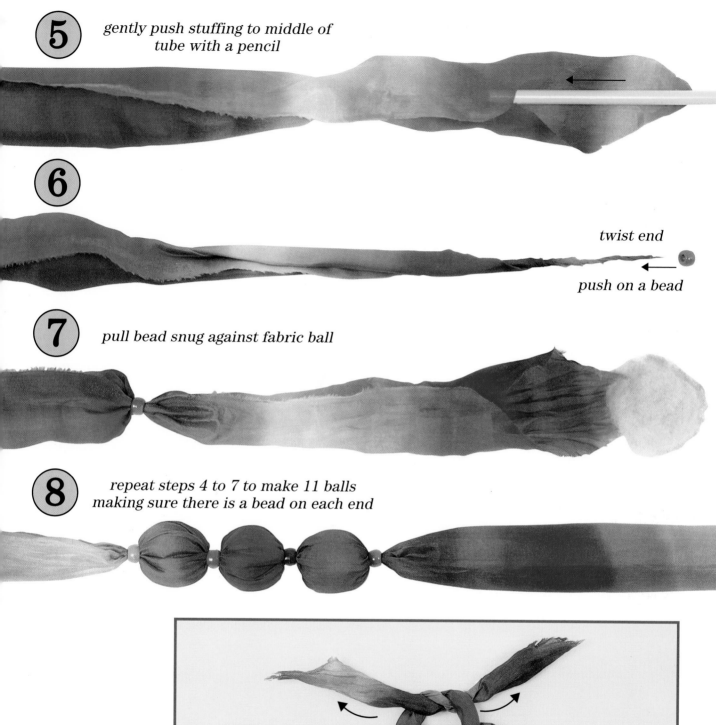

6 *twist end*

push on a bead

7 *pull bead snug against fabric ball*

8 *repeat steps 4 to 7 to make 11 balls making sure there is a bead on each end*

9 *tie ends together to fasten*

PRECIOUS PETS

POUCH

- knit fabric
- chalk
- scissors
- hole punch
- shoelace

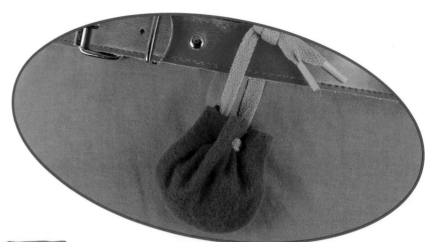

1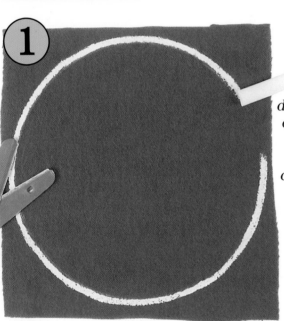

draw a circle

cut out

2

punch an even number of holes around edge

3

thread shoelace in and out of holes

4

pull shoelace to gather fabric into pouch

tie ends together

PETS

- small smooth stones
- paper
- pencil crayons
- acrylic paint and brush

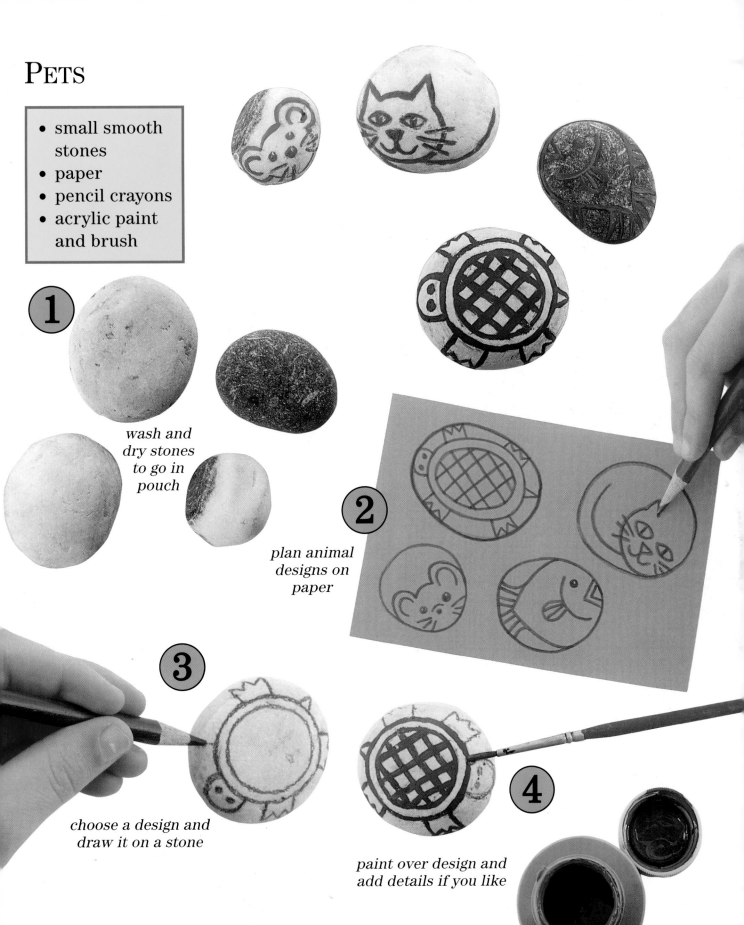

1 wash and dry stones to go in pouch

2 plan animal designs on paper

3 choose a design and draw it on a stone

4 paint over design and add details if you like

JEWELRY BOX

- shoe box with hinged lid
- acrylic paint
- paintbrush
- egg carton
- scissors
- white glue
- aluminum foil
- hole punch
- 2 long pieces of ribbon
- 2 short pieces of ribbon
- pencil
- button
- *grown-up to help*

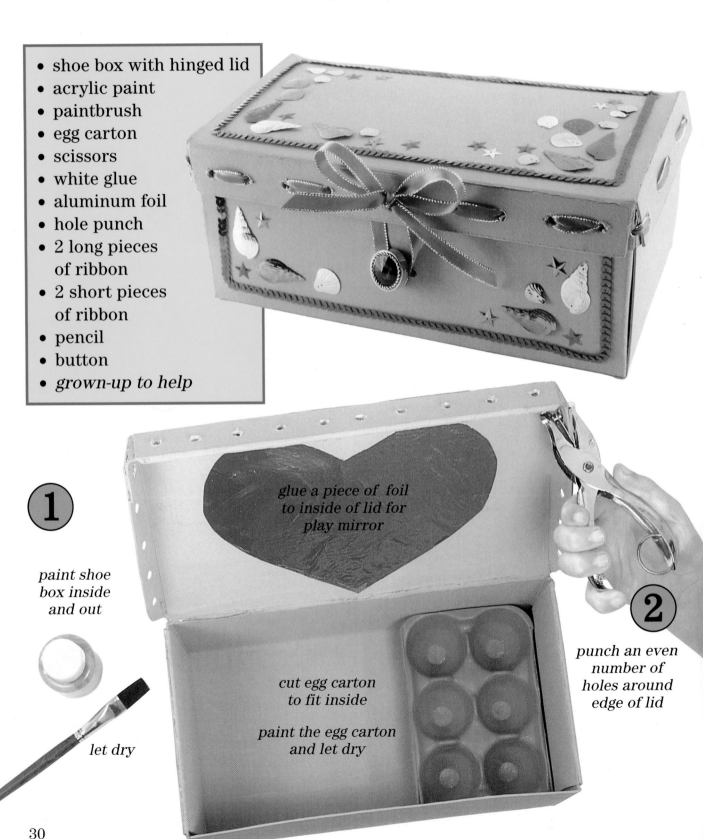

1 paint shoe box inside and out

let dry

glue a piece of foil to inside of lid for play mirror

cut egg carton to fit inside

paint the egg carton and let dry

2 punch an even number of holes around edge of lid

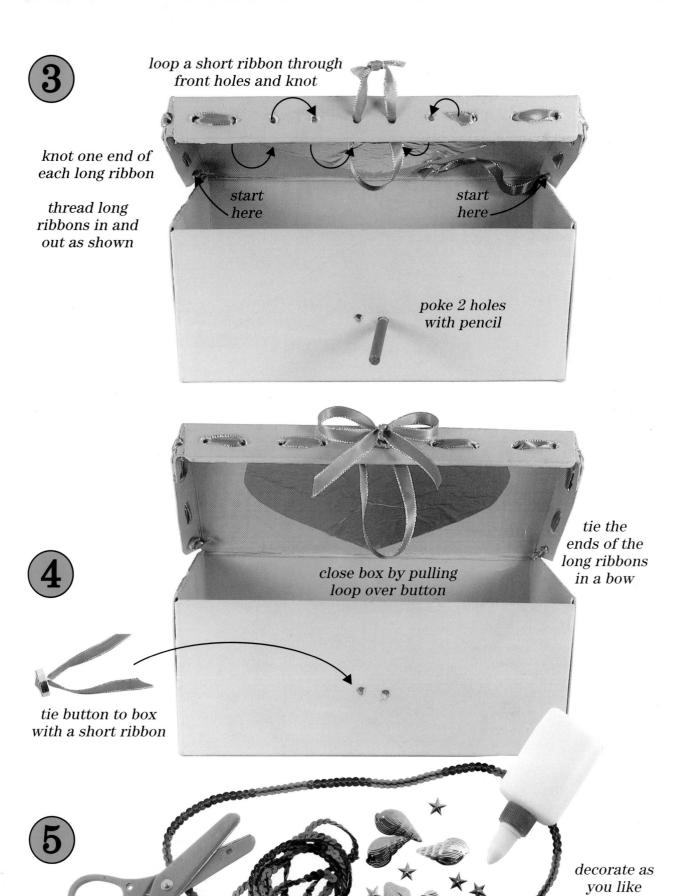

3

loop a short ribbon through front holes and knot

knot one end of each long ribbon

thread long ribbons in and out as shown

start here

start here

poke 2 holes with pencil

4

close box by pulling loop over button

tie the ends of the long ribbons in a bow

tie button to box with a short ribbon

5

decorate as you like